WILD

Sierra V Cast

Photography By Sierra V Cast

Edited By Summer L Cast and Maryanne M Mattson

ISBN:1501033956
ISBN-13: 978-1501033957

FORWARD

This is the true story of four wild horses and their journey to safety after being taken from their home. In 2012, the Nevada Forrest Service rounded up 145 wild horses occupying land not under the protection of the Bureau of Land Management (BLM). Because they were occupying this land, they were not under the security of the Wild Horse Act, which prevents wild horses from being taken to slaughter. Traps were set for the horses, and after being caught, they were taken to a holding pen, where the mares, foals, and stallions were all separated. The horses were branded with an "N" for the state of Nevada, and all of the stallions were gelded. After this was done, the horses were brought to the Fallon sale barn, all of them destined for slaughter. Fortunately, the Virginia Range Wild Horse Protection Fund received news of what had happened and was able to raise enough money to buy all 145 horses. They were sent either to foster homes or to the Wynema Ranch Wild Horse Sanctuary in California, and many of the families were never reunited. However, because of their unique coloring, the family of crèmes, Celine, Sinatra, and Butter, as later named by Vendla Stockdale, co-founder of Spirit Wind Horse Rescue, were reunited at the Wynema Ranch. They remained at the ranch for two years, adopting into their band a sorrel gelding named River, who acted as their protector. In 2014, the four horses were permanently adopted by Cindy A. Lee of the Wags and Menace Make A Difference Foundation, and brought to the Spirit Wind Horse Rescue in Hotchkiss, Colorado, where they will remain for the rest of their lives.

"Each year, more than 100,000 American horses—working, racing and companion horses and even children's ponies—are inhumanely transported long distances in cramped trailers without food, water or rest. Then they are brutally slaughtered, and their meat is shipped overseas for human consumption. The majority of these horses are young, healthy animals who could have led productive lives with loving owners if they'd been given the chance." (The Humane Society of The United States) Neglectful and abusive owners who no longer can, or no longer want to take care of their horses, ship them off to sale barns for a cruel and horrific fate. Wild horses living on unregulated lands are rounded up, crammed into trailers, and sent to slaughter. Some of these beautiful creatures are fortunate enough to be rescued, but still thousands suffer a terrible and despicable fate. There is no humane way to slaughter a horse, and in most cases, it is done in an entirely inhumane way. Because of their size, accurate stunning is difficult to achieve, and most horses suffer repeated blows before they are stunned, or simply remain conscious for slaughter and dismemberment. Once killed, the horsemeat is shipped overseas for consumption. Until 2007, horsemeat was also consumed in the US, until the USDA (United States Department of Agriculture) banned its usage in commercial food products due to the safety violations it presented, being that horses are raised as companion animals and are usually administered numerous toxic substances for medical concerns throughout their lives. Although domestic slaughter is no longer legal in the United States since 2007, thousands upon thousands of our horses are still being transported across borders to die. Kill buyers frequent the sale barns where unwanted horses are sent, looking to buy the horses and ship them to a slaughterhouse or feedlot. The entirety of the slaughter process is not only despicable and inhumane, but it is also unnecessary. "There are several ways to address homeless horse issues. We can limit overbreeding, provide shelter, and expand adoption work. More than 160,000 horses were sent to slaughter in 2013 alone, and a vast majority of them would have been good candidates for new homes. The USDA documented that 92.3 percent of horses sent to slaughter are in good condition and are able to live out a productive life. These horses could be sold, donated, or otherwise rehomed; however, kill buyers regularly outbid legitimate horse owners and rescues at auctions. Using the USDA's finding, the number of horses sent to slaughter that may require humane euthanasia is a fraction of a percent of the entire horse population. The idea of slaughtering companion animals is unacceptable to the American people and will never be embraced. A 2012 national poll found that 80 percent of Americans support a ban on horse slaughter for human consumption. There are countries that consume dogs, cats, and other pets as food, but we do not allow our dogs and cats to be exported for food purposes, even though pet overpopulation is a well-documented problem. Horse slaughter enables and perpetrates overbreeding, neglect, and irresponsibility. As long as breeders can sell their unwanted horses to slaughter, they will be rewarded for overbreeding—and they will continue. Horse slaughter is purely a function of supply and demand, not a disposal service." (The Humane Society of The United States) There are also many economical concerns surrounding horse slaughter, as its practice diverts financial resources away from food safety and products purposed for the US. In 2013, the USDA restored the authority to fund inspections of horse slaughter meat and slaughter facilities. This is an expensive process that pulls millions of dollars out of food safety programs in the US in order to enable a practice that is opposed by 80% of Americans. Because of the evidence that the drugs administered to US horses is dangerous for human consumption, the cost of these inspections will only rise in years to come, so now is the time to speak up and make a difference.

It is time to take measures to help to end these horrible actions against our beloved American horses. There are so many ways to help these beautiful creatures destined for slaughter. Small ways to make a difference can be as simple as writing a letter to your legislators informing them of the cruelty and disadvantages of horse slaughter. Donating money to a local or national horse rescue or foundation can make huge differences in the number of horses able to be rescued. Raising public awareness of the issue and encouraging others to act against this travesty could change the tides for these horses. Other ways to help include volunteering time at a nearby horse shelter or adopting your own rescue horse. The facts are clear: horse slaughter needs to end, and it is up to our US citizens to make the difference and create the change. Below is information about the Homes For Horses Coalition, an organization co-founded by the Humane Society of the United States that is "a group of welfare and equine rescue organizations dedicated to ending horse slaughter and equine abuse as well as promoting collaboration and professionalism in the equine rescue community." (Homes For Horses Coalition)

Homes For Horses Coalition

Website: www.homesforhorses.org

Email: info@homesforhorses.org

This coalition is a great way to get connected with horse rescues and make a difference!

The journey of Spirit Wind Horse Rescue's family of wild horses as written from the perspective of the mother and mare, Celine.

I remember the way dust flurried up around us as we moved forward as one. The particles rose, dancing through the still, hot air until they separated and settled behind us, like awoken spirits sent back to rest. I remember the way the sagebrush bit into the dry earth, a vestige of life in the quiet desert. I remember the hot sun that filled every valley with golden light, pouring like water over the hills in the early morning hours. I remember the damp and soothing smell of long-dead wood after a day of clouds and rain. This beautiful land was our home, our place of belonging and freedom.

There, in our home, I didn't have to see my family, my herd, to know they were beside me. If I closed my eyes, I felt the heartbeat of their hooves upon the ground. The wind when we ran pushed through my body, calling out to us as we moved together like an exhilarated force of life. We ran for freedom, we ran for the wind, we ran for the love of running free. The days would bloom before our eager eyes like the petals of a spring flower. Every moment we relished, cherished, and spent as one; my brothers, my sisters, my child, my mate, my family. When we ran we were a single being, flying like an eagle across the desert ground, powerful and free. We are the wild, and we are the strong.

It was when the sun began her decent that we found the cage; metal bars housing food and water. Perhaps our thirsty bones knew better, perhaps our famished mouths were foolish, but we moved forward anyway, and the cage closed behind us. I could see from their eyes that the others knew we had been wrong to enter. I could see the faint traces of regret, but we ate and drank and waited all the same. I remember the men who looked at us with hungry eyes and took us from our home.

The morning was filled with voices, shouting men with loud machines who gazed at our bodies and forgot about our souls. There was fear now, around me and inside of me, crackling through the air. Our children cried out, seeking a comfort that no longer existed. Hooves pounded the ground, seeking solidity as it slid from beneath us. We were trapped as they descended upon us like vultures, picking the freedom from our bones. We were pushed into the humming beasts, crying out as the men with hungry eyes drove us forward with stings like licks of fire from long and cracking whips. We were forced into those metal mouths, where there was no sky, and there was no ground, and there would never again be freedom.

My baby stood beside me, and I knew I could do nothing, for there is no comfort in captivity. My mate pressed against me with his beating heart and panicked breath, sending shivers through my bones. I saw my family through metal slates and imprisonment, I saw the fear, I felt the struggle. But the growling machines with their glowing eyes leapt forward and my home faded away into unfamiliar places full of acrid smells and tainted feelings.

Time crawled forward carrying a stiffening anticipation I'd never felt before. The vibrating ground of the metal beast disguised my shaking legs, but my eyes could not conceal my fear. Panic drove its way into my veins like a poison, strangling my hope and erasing my courage. With a jolt, the beast ceased movement, and darkness descended. The air was filled with the cries of my family, the scent of blood and burning, sweat and terror. The clanging sounds of my pacing hooves joined the dreadful symphony as I waited for what was to come. What was to come?

Light suddenly filled the metal cage, bringing images to my eyes as hands pulled me forward, stole my child, ripped apart my family. All around me was suffering, movement and pain. I fought against the hands, but biting ropes stung my skin and choked my neck. My eyes were wide, but disbelief blinded me as I fought to run. Where was my child? Where was he? More hands, more metal bars, more biting ropes. My mouth was filled with the taste of hot air and undeniable fear. My throat felt raw as I joined the chorus of screaming. Shaking bodies pressed against me and knocked into my ribs as the hands moved us forward. Forward into metal bars that dug into my side and held me prisoner.

Forward when the men had finished burning my skin with searing metal. Forward into a new cage full of crumpled spirits. Forward into nothing.

The sun rose and fell, rose and fell, and we waited. I stood with the other mothers and mares, looking into their desolate eyes knowing they were only reflecting my own. We called out for our children, we called out for our mates, we called out for the wind that once sang through our bodies. The men came and left, leaving disquiet food and remorseful water. Breathe in, we wait, breathe out, we call. Rising, falling, rising, falling. Feed our disquiet, quench our remorse. Rising, falling, rising, falling. Call out to the empty feelings and sickening hopes in our stomachs. Rising, falling. The humming beasts return.

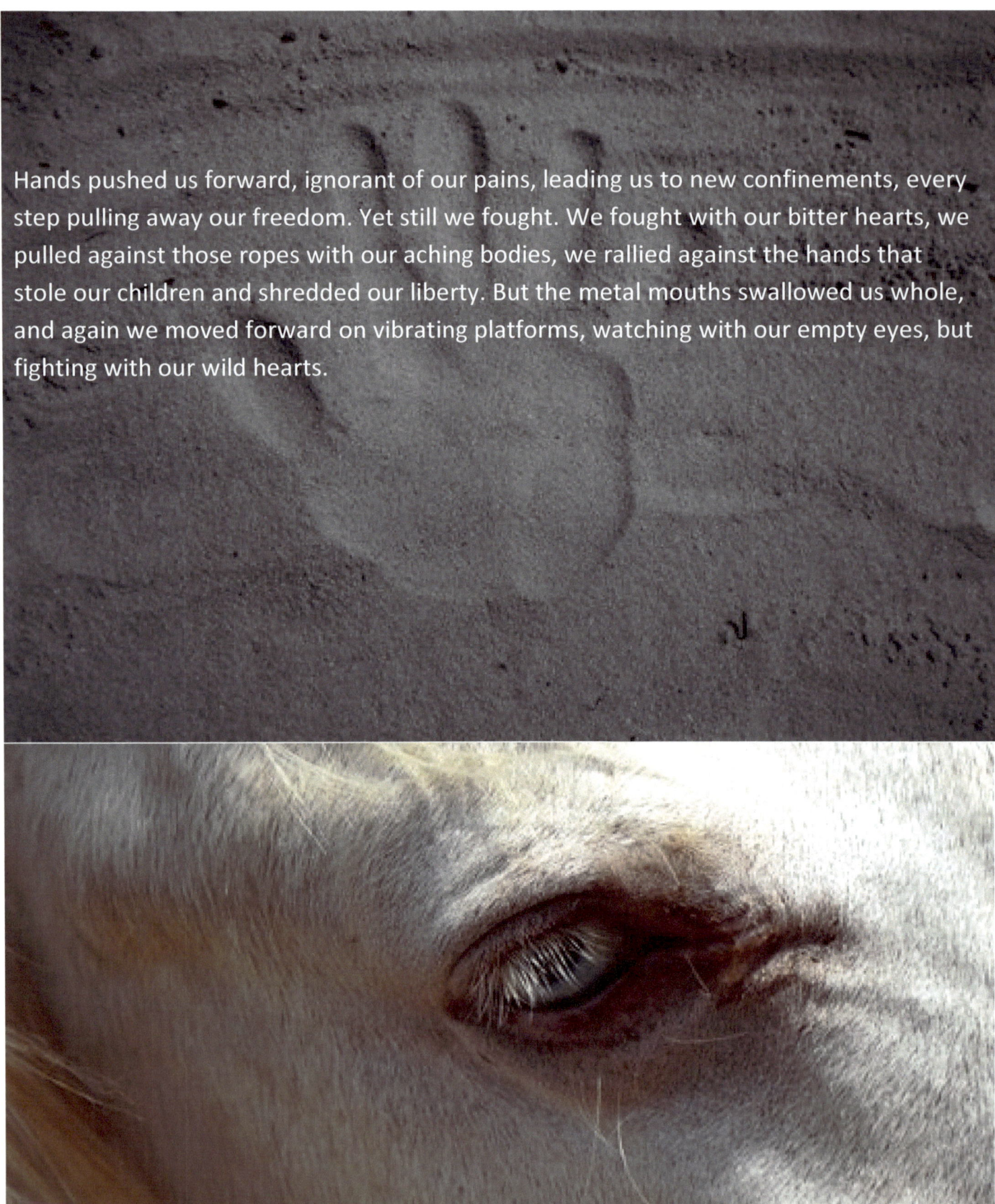

Hands pushed us forward, ignorant of our pains, leading us to new confinements, every step pulling away our freedom. Yet still we fought. We fought with our bitter hearts, we pulled against those ropes with our aching bodies, we rallied against the hands that stole our children and shredded our liberty. But the metal mouths swallowed us whole, and again we moved forward on vibrating platforms, watching with our empty eyes, but fighting with our wild hearts.

You never forget the smell of death, or the feeling it brands on the earth and air. The metal mouth spat us out onto a land burned and bleeding death. We stood and moved through the cages in shock, slowly progressing towards what lay ahead. The quiet that sometimes descended was so loud it drowned us. We moved between the metal as humans stared and pointed, shouted and argued. These hours would decide our fate. One hundred and forty five of us stood and waited to die or live. The air surrounding us became electric with anticipation, fear, and confusion. The devastation was tangible, but you could still feel the hope. Hope for life. Hope for release. Hope for hope. What more could those hungry eyes take from us? What more did we have to give?

Our tired breathing stretched on while the sun crossed the sky and metal mouths swallowed pieces of my family, taking them to places I will never know. Then it is my turn to disappear, to leave my family behind in this place of death and destruction. There is a numbness that invades my thoughts, slowly dimming the noises around me until only my panting breath fills my ears. Again, I am loaded into the metal mouth of a human machine. Through the gaps in the metal I watch my family fade into the past.

When the beast is finally quiet, I am led into another enclosure, another cage. But the hands and faces that guide me are gentle; the feeling of this place is kind, but my wary heart is not quick to trust. I stand, and again, I wait, closing my eyes to the cruel sun, watching the memories flash through my personal darkness. I can still hear my child call out to me, I can still feel the familiar beat of my families hooves upon the ground, still smell their sweat and longing breath. When my eyes open, the hands are guiding my baby towards me, the hands are bringing me my mate. My feet stomp the ground as time carries them forward. There is a hope that rushes through me; a feeling that I thought had abandoned me. My voice joins theirs as the cage opens to them, the metal closing behind them, holding us together. I cannot know the horrors they felt, but it begins to melt away with every touch, every look, and every glorious moment of being together again. I swallow my fears and succumb to relief. Wherever we go, we are here together, unbroken.

There are others at this new place, and their eyes tell stories of time and memory. There is a watchfulness among us - a seclusion. Things are different, we are all changed, we are all branded, we have all suffered loss. But we keep apart, afraid to gain too much, to have more to lose. Here it feels like standing on melting ice, watching the cracks appear, and waiting for the plunge. My family stays close together, afraid to stand apart for even a briefest moment, afraid of the hands that hold the possibility of tearing us apart once more.

There is one who walks alone, one with fierce and quiet eyes. He watches us, but never approaches.

In time we accept him as our own, because there is not a single joy in walking this earth alone. His fierce and quiet eyes protect us. There is a strength in him that can only be felt, for some things are not meant to be seen.

Time trudges forward like a lost and lonely child, looking for signs of familiarity, but finding only obscurity. We wait here, unknowing, until the metal mouths come again. Change lights the horizon as the four of us travel together, always together, towards the very last stop.

We stand side by side within the metal bars, peace and calmness igniting the air with eternal hope. A woman walks towards us, watching with blue eyes and curiosity. She speaks to us, and though we do not know her words, we feel them. Like light in our hearts, we feel them. There will be no more pain. There will be no more suffering. There will be no more separation. There will be only love. Only family. Only here. Always and forever.

I often think of my freedom, my homeland, of running with the wind and wild horses. I know that this is the last stop on our journey, that my family will travel no further, but this place, with all of its comforts, will never be our home. The people here look at us and know. Perhaps they have done us a justice by giving us a sanctuary from the hungry eyed men. Perhaps they have given us a new life, a new hope, a new beginning. But at night, when it is just the stars above and the ground below, the wind whispers through the leaves, calling out to us to remember who we are. We are the wild. We are the strong.

End Word

Written by Vendla Stockdale

Co-Founder of Spirit Wind Horse Rescue

Sitting in a sale barn for the first time and watching so many countless beautiful horses being run through and headed for slaughter, was what began my dream of wanting to make a difference. It was a young sorrel filly with big brown eyes that stared directly at me with a plea for help that changed the world for all the horses that have found safe haven through our rescue. Her name was Manzie, meaning water, and even though she has moved on to greener pastures and now leads our herd in the sky, it was because of her that the Crèmes now have a safe place to call home. Cindy A. Lee of the Wags and Menace Make a Difference Foundation has helped save many, many mustangs from slaughter, and has permanently adopted the Crème family. It is rare that wild horses are kept together as a family unit, but because of Cindy and her foundation, this family of four will live forever under the shadows of the beautiful West Elk Mountains with green pastures where they will never have to face being separated ever again. They will never have to face the sale barn where no doubt they would disappear into the slaughter pipeline; just a memory of blue eyes the color of the Caribbean Sea and manes blowing in the wind. Now, here at Spirit Wind Horse Rescue, we get to watch them grow in their new human world.

CONTACT PAGE

Spirit Wind Horse Rescue

Website:
www.spiritwindhorserescue.com

Email: spiritwind@tds.net

Phone: (970) 921-5646

(970) 589-2172

Mailing Address:

Beth Keenan, Co-Founder

Spirit Wind Horse Rescue

P.O. Box 27

Hotchkiss, CO 81419

Wags and Menace Make A Difference Foundation

Website: www.wagsandmenace.org

Phone: (303) 300-6881

Mailing Address:

Wags and Menace Make A Difference Foundation

1330 S Glencoe St.

Denver, CO 80222

Virginia Range Wild Horse Protection Fund

Website: www.hiddenvalleyhorses.com

Email:
hiddenvalleywildhorses@gmail.com

Wynema Ranch Wild Horse Sanctuary

Website: www.wynemaranch.com

Email: wynemaranch@gmail.com

Phone: (775) 842-6229

Mailing Address:

Shari Floyd

P.O. Box 12787

Reno, NV 89510

Homes For Horses Coalition

Website: www.homesforhorses.org

Email: info@homesforhorses.org

Humane Society of The United States

Website: www.humanesociety.org

Phone: (202) 452-1100

(866) 720-2676

Mailing Address:

The Humane Society of The United States

2100 L St., NW

Washington D.C. 20037